THE CHILDREN'S SHAKESPEARE

Viola: "My Lord and Master loves you"

E. NESBIT

The Children's
SHAKESPEARE

ILLUSTRATED BY ROLF KLEP

Academy Chicago Publishers

Academy Chicago Publishers
363 West Erie Street
Chicago, Illinois 60610

Printed and bound in the U.S.A.
First Academy Chicago Edition 2000.
11 10 09 08 07   2 3 4 5 6

Library of Congress Cataloging-in-Publication Data

Nesbit, E. (Edith), 1858–1924.
    The children's Shakespeare / E. Nesbit ; illustrated by Rolf Klep.
        p. cm.
    ISBN 0-89733-485-X
    1. Shakespeare, William, 1564–1616.—Adaptations—Juvenile literature.
  [1. Shakespeare, William, 1564–1616—Adaptations.] I. Klep, Rolf, ill.
  II. Shakespeare, William, 1564–1616. Plays. Selections. III. Title.

    PR2877.B5   20000
    822'.912—dc12   00-044199

Contents

Illustrations

Introduction

It was evening. The fire burned brightly in the inn parlor. We had been that day to see Shakespeare's house, and I had told the children all that I could about him and his work. Now they were sitting by the table, poring over a big volume of the Master's plays, lent them by the landlord. And I, with eyes fixed on the fire, was wandering happily in the immortal dreamland peopled by Rosalind and Imogen, Lear and Hamlet. A small sigh roused me.

"I can't understand a word of it," said Iris.

"And you said it was so beautiful," Rosamund added, reproachfully. "What does it all mean?"

"Yes," Iris went on, "you said it was a fairy tale, and we've read three pages, and there's nothing about fairies, not even a dwarf, or a fairy god-mother."

"And what does 'misgraffed' mean?"

"And 'vantage,' and 'austerity,' and 'belike,' and 'edict,' and—"

"Stop, stop," I cried; "I will tell you the story."

In a moment they were nestling beside me, cooing with the pleasure that the promise of a story always brings them.

"But you must be quiet a moment, and let me think."

In truth it was not easy to arrange the story simply. Even with the recollection of Lamb's tales to help me I found it hard to tell the "Midsummer Night's Dream" in words that these little ones could understand. But presently I began the tale, and then the words came fast enough. When the story was ended, Iris drew a long breath.

"It is a lovely story," she said; "but it doesn't look at all like that in the book."

"It is only put differently," I answered. "You will understand when you grow up that the stories are the least part of Shakespeare."

"But it's the stories we like," said Rosamund.

"You see he did not write for children."

"No, but you might," cried Iris, flushed with a sudden idea. "Why don't you write the stories for us so that we can understand them, just as you told us that, and then, when we are grown up, we shall understand the plays so much better. Do! do!"

"Ah, do! You will, won't you? You must!"

"Oh, well, if I must, I must," I said.

And so they settled it for me, and for them these tales were written.

THE CHILDREN'S SHAKESPEARE

Prince Florizel meets Perdita

The Winter's Tale

LEONTES was the King of Sicily, and his dearest friend was Polixenes, King of Bohemia. They had been brought up together and only separated when they reached man's estate and each had to go and rule over his kingdom. After many years, when each was married and had a son, Polixenes came to stay with Leontes in Sicily.

Leontes was a violent-tempered man and rather silly, and he took it into his stupid head that his wife, Hermione, liked Polixenes better than she did him, her own husband. When once he had got this into his head, nothing could put it out; and he ordered one of his lords, Camillo, to put a poison in Polixenes' wine. Camillo tried to dissuade him from this wicked action, but finding he was not to be moved, pretended to consent. He then told Polixenes what was proposed against him, and they fled from the Court of Sicily that night, and returned to Bohemia where Camillo lived on as Polixenes' friend and counselor.

Leontes threw the Queen into prison; and her son, the heir

to the throne, died of sorrow to see his mother so unjustly and cruelly treated.

While the Queen was in prison she had a little baby, and a friend of hers, named Paulina, had the baby dressed in its best, and took it to show the King, thinking that the sight of his helpless little daughter would soften his heart towards his dear Queen, who had never done him any wrong, and who loved him a great deal more than he deserved; but the King would not look at the baby, and ordered Paulina's husband to take it away in a ship, and leave it in the most desert and dreadful place he could find, which Paulina's husband, very much against his will, was obliged to do.

Then the poor Queen was brought up to be tried for treason in preferring Polixenes to her King; but really she had never thought of anyone except Leontes, her husband. Leontes had sent some messengers to ask the god, Apollo, whether he was not right in his cruel thoughts of the Queen. But he had not patience to wait till they came back, and so it happened that they arrived in the middle of the trial. The Oracle said:

"Hermione is innocent, Polixenes blameless, Camillo a true subject, Leontes a jealous tyrant, and the King shall live without an heir, if that which is lost be not found."

Then a man came and told them that the little prince was dead. The poor Queen, hearing this, fell down in a fit; and then the King saw how wicked and wrong he had been. He ordered Paulina and the ladies who were with the Queen to take her away, and try to restore her. But Paulina came back in a few moments, and told the King that Hermione was dead.

Now Leontes' eyes were at last open to his folly. His Queen was dead, and the little daughter who might have been a comfort to him he had sent away to be the prey of wolves and kites. Life had nothing left for him now. He gave himself up to his grief, and passed many sad years in prayer and remorse.

The baby Princess was left on the sea-coast of Bohemia, the very kingdom where Polixenes reigned. Paulina's husband never went home to tell Leontes where he had left the baby; for as he was going back to the ship, he met a bear and was torn to pieces. So there was an end of him.

But the poor, deserted little baby was found by a shepherd. She was richly dressed, and had with her some jewels, and a paper was pinned to her cloak, saying that her name was Perdita, and that she came of noble parents.

The shepherd, being a kind-hearted man, took home the little baby to his wife, and they brought it up as their own child. She had no more teaching than a shepherd's child generally has, but she inherited from her royal mother many graces and charms, so that she was quite different from the other maidens in the village where she lived.

One day Prince Florizel, the son of the good King of Bohemia, was hunting near the shepherd's house and saw Perdita, now grown up to a charming woman. He made friends with the shepherd, not telling him that he was the Prince, but saying that his name was Doricles, and that he was a private gentleman; and then, being deeply in love with the pretty Perdita, he came almost daily to see her.

The King could not understand what it was that took his son nearly every day from home; so he set people to watch him, and then found out that the heir of the King of Bohemia was in love with Perdita, the pretty shepherd girl. Polixenes, wishing to see whether this was true, disguised himself, and went with the faithful Camillo, in disguise too, to the old shepherd's house. They arrived at the feast of sheep-shearing, and, though strangers, they were made very welcome. There was dancing going on, and a peddler was selling ribbons and laces and gloves, which the young men bought for their sweethearts.

Florizel and Perdita, however, were taking no part in this gay scene, but sat quietly together talking. The King noticed the charming manners and great beauty of Perdita, never guessing that she was the daughter of his old friend, Leontes. He said to Camillo:

"This is the prettiest low-born lass that ever ran on the

green sward. Nothing she does or seems but smacks of something greater than herself—too noble for this place."

And Camillo answered, "In truth she is the Queen of curds and cream."

But when Florizel, who did not recognize his father, called upon the strangers to witness his betrothal with the pretty shepherdess, the King made himself known and forbade the marriage, adding, that if she ever saw Florizel again, he would kill her and her old father, the shepherd; and with that he left them. But Camillo remained behind, for he was charmed with Perdita, and wished to befriend her.

Camillo had long known how sorry Leontes was for that foolish madness of his, and he longed to go back to Sicily to see his old master. He now proposed that the young people should go there and claim the protection of Leontes. So they went, and the shepherd went with them, taking Perdita's jewels, her baby clothes, and the paper he had found pinned to her cloak.

Leontes received them with great kindness. He was very polite to Prince Florizel, but all his looks were for Perdita. He saw how much she was like the Queen Hermione, and said again and again:

"Such a sweet creature my daughter might have been, if I had not cruelly sent her from me."

When the old shepherd heard that the King had lost a baby daughter, who had been left upon the coast of Bohemia, he felt sure that Perdita, the child he had reared, must be the King's daughter, and when he told his tale and showed the jewels and the paper, the King perceived that Perdita was indeed his long-lost child. He welcomed her with joy, and rewarded the good shepherd.

Polixenes had hastened after his son to prevent his marriage with Perdita, but when he found that she was the daughter of his old friend, he was only too glad to give his consent.

Yet Leontes could not be happy. He remembered how his fair queen, who should have been at his side to share his joy in his daughter's happiness, was dead through his unkindness, and he could say nothing for a long time but:

"Oh, thy mother! thy mother!" and ask forgiveness of the King of Bohemia, and then kiss his daughter again, and then the Prince Florizel, and then thank the old shepherd for all his goodness.

Then Paulina, who had been high all these years in the King's favor, because of her kindness to the dead Queen Hermione, said, "I have a statue made in the likeness of the dead queen, a piece many years in doing, and performed by the rare Italian Master, Giulio Romano. I keep it in a private house apart, and there, ever since you lost your queen, I have gone twice or thrice a day. Will it please your Majesty to go and see the statue?"

So Leontes, and Polixenes, and Florizel, and Perdita, with Camillo and their attendants, went to Paulina's house, and there was a heavy purple curtain screening off an alcove; and Paulina, with her hand on the curtain, said:

"She was peerless when she was alive, and I do believe that her dead likeness excels whatever yet you have looked upon, or that the hand of man hath done. Therefore I keep it lonely, apart. But here it is. Behold, and say 'tis well."

And with that she drew back the curtain and showed them the statue. The King gazed and gazed on the beautiful statue of his dead wife, but said nothing.

"I like your silence," said Paulina, "it the more shows off your wonder; but speak, is it not like her?"

"It is almost herself," said the King, "and yet, Paulina, Hermione was not so much wrinkled, nothing like so old as this seems."

"Oh, not by much," said Polixenes.

"Ah," said Paulina, "that is the cleverness of the carver, who shows her to us as she would have been, had she lived till now."

And still Leontes looked at the statue and could not take his eyes away.

"If I had known," said Paulina, "that this poor image would so have stirred your grief, and love, I would not have shown it to you."

But he only answered, "Do not draw the curtain."

"No, you must not look any longer," said Paulina, "or you will think it moves."

"Let be, let be!" said the King. "Would you not think it breathed?"

"I will draw the curtain," said Paulina, "you will think it lives presently."

"Ah, sweet Paulina," said Leontes, "make me to think so twenty years together."

"If you can bear it," said Paulina, "I can make the statue move, make it come down and take you by the hand. Only you would think it was by wicked magic."

"Whatever you can make her do, I am content to look on," said the King. And then, all folks there admiring and beholding, the statue moved from its pedestal, and came down the steps and put its arms round the King's neck, and he held her face and kissed her many times, for this was no statue, but the real living Queen Hermione herself. She had lived, hidden by Paulina's kindness, all these years, and would not have discovered herself to her husband, though she knew he had repented, because she could not quite forgive him till she knew what had become of her little baby. Now that Perdita was found, she forgave her husband everything, and it was like a new and beautiful marriage to them, to be together once more. Florizel and Perdita were married, and lived long and happily. To Leontes his long years of suffering were well paid for, in the moment, when, after long grief and pain, he felt the arms of his true love round him once again.

Romeo: "Eyes, look your last!"

Romeo and Juliet

ONCE upon a time there lived in Verona two great families named Montagu and Capulet. They were both rich, and I suppose they were as sensible, in most things, as other rich people. But in one thing they were extremely silly. There was an old, old quarrel between the two families, and instead of making it up like reasonable folks, they made a sort of pet of their quarrel, and would not let it die out. So that a Montagu wouldn't speak to a Capulet if he met one in the street—nor a Capulet to a Montagu—or if they did speak, it was to say rude and unpleasant things, which often ended in a fight. And their relations and servants were just as foolish, so that street fights and duels and uncomfortablenesses of that kind were always growing out of the Montagu-and-Capulet quarrel.

Now Lord Capulet, the head of that family, gave a party—a grand supper and dance—and he was so hospitable that he said anyone might come to it—*except* (of course) the Montagues. But there was a young Montagu named Romeo, who very much wanted to be there, because Rosaline, the lady he loved, had been asked. This lady had never been at all kind to him, and he had no reason to love her; but the fact was that he wanted to love *somebody*, and as he hadn't seen the right lady, he was obliged to love the wrong one. So to the Capulets' grand party he came, with his friends Mercutio and Benvolio.

Old Capulet welcomed him and his two friends very kindly —and young Romeo moved about among the crowd of courtly folk dressed in their velvets and satins, the men with jeweled sword hilts and collars, and the ladies with brilliant gems on breast and arms, and stones of price set in their bright girdles. Romeo was in his best too, and though he wore a black mask over his eyes and nose, every one could see by his mouth and his hair, and the way he held his head, that he was twelve times handsomer than any one else in the room.

Presently amid the dancers he saw a lady so beautiful and so lovable, that from that moment he never again gave one thought to that Rosaline whom he had thought he loved. And he looked at this other fair lady, as she moved in the dance in her white satin and pearls, and all the world seemed vain and worthless to him compared with her. And he was saying this—or something like it—to his friend, when Tybalt, Lady Capulet's nephew, hearing his voice, knew him to be Romeo. Tybalt, being very angry, went at once to his uncle,

and told him how a Montagu had come uninvited to the feast;
but old Capulet was too fine a gentleman to be discourteous
to any man under his own roof, and he bade Tybalt be quiet.
But this young man only waited for a chance to quarrel with
Romeo.

In the meantime Romeo made his way to the fair lady, and
told her in sweet words that he loved her, and kissed her. Just
then her mother sent for her, and then Romeo found out that
the lady on whom he had set his heart's hopes was Juliet, the
daughter of Lord Capulet, his **sworn foe**. So he went away,
sorrowing indeed, but loving her none the less.

Then Juliet said to her nurse:

"Who is that gentleman that would not dance?"

"His name is Romeo, and a Montagu, the only son of your
great enemy," answered the nurse.

Then Juliet went to her room, and looked out of her window over the beautiful green-gray garden, where the moon
was shining. And Romeo was hidden in that garden among the
trees—because he could not bear to go right away without
trying to see her again. So she—not knowing him to be there
—spoke her secret thought aloud, and told the quiet garden
how she loved Romeo.

And Romeo heard and was glad beyond measure; hidden
below, he looked up and saw her fair face in the moonlight,

framed in the blossoming creepers that grew round her window, and as he looked and listened, he felt as though he had been carried away in a dream, and set down by some magician in that beautiful and enchanted garden.

"Ah—why are you called Romeo?" said Juliet. "Since I love you, what does it matter what you are called?"

"Call me but love, and I'll be new baptized—henceforth I never will be Romeo," he cried, stepping into the full white moonlight from the shade of the cypressses and oleanders that had hidden him. She was frightened at first, but when she saw that it was Romeo himself, and no stranger, she too was glad, and, he standing in the garden below and she leaning from the window, they spoke long together, each one trying to find the sweetest words in the world, to make that pleasant talk that lovers use. And the tale of all they said, and the sweet music their voices made together, is all set down in a golden book, where you children may read it for yourselves some day.

And the time passed so quickly, as it does for folk who love each other and are together, that when the time came to part, it seemed as though they had met but that moment—and indeed they hardly knew how to part.

"I will send to you tomorrow," said Juliet.

And so at last, with lingering and longing, they said good-bye.

Juliet went into her room, and a dark curtain hid her bright window. Romeo went away through the still and dewy garden like a man in a dream.

The next morning very early Romeo went to Friar Laurence, a priest, and, telling him all the story, begged him to marry him to Juliet without delay. And this, after some talk, the priest consented to do.

So when Juliet sent her old nurse to Romeo that day to know what he purposed to do, the old woman took back a message that all was well, and all things ready for the marriage of Juliet and Romeo on the next morning.

The young lovers were afraid to ask their parents' consent to their marriage, as young people should do, because of this foolish old quarrel between the Capulets and the Montagues.

And Friar Laurence was willing to help the young lovers secretly, because he thought that when they were once married their parents might soon be told, and that the match might put a happy end to the old quarrel.

So the next morning early, Romeo and Juliet were married at Friar Laurence's cell, and parted with tears and kisses. And Romeo promised to come into the garden that evening, and the nurse got ready a rope-ladder to let down from the window, so that Romeo could climb up and talk to his dear wife quietly and alone.

But that very day a dreadful thing happened.

Tybalt, the young man who had been so vexed at Romeo's going to the Capulets' feast, met him and his two friends, Mercutio and Benvolio, in the street, called Romeo a villain, and asked him to fight. Romeo had no wish to fight with Juliet's cousin, but Mercutio drew his sword, and he and Tybalt fought. And Mercutio was killed. When Romeo saw that his friend was dead he forgot everything, except anger at the man who had killed him, and he and Tybalt fought, till Tybalt fell dead. So, on the very day of his wedding, Romeo killed his dear Juliet's cousin, and was sentenced to be banished. Poor Juliet and her young husband met that night indeed; he climbed the rope-ladder among the flowers, and found her window, but their meeting was a sad one, and they parted with bitter tears and hearts heavy, because they could not know when they should meet again.

Now Juliet's father, who, of course, had no idea that she was married, wished her to wed a gentleman named Paris, and was so angry when she refused, that she hurried away to ask Friar Laurence what she should do. He advised her to pretend to consent, and then he said:

"I will give you a draught that will make you seem to be dead for two days, and then when they take you to church it will be to bury you, and not to marry you. They will put you in the vault thinking you are dead, and before you wake up Romeo and I will be there to take care of you. Will you do this, or are you afraid?"

"I will do it; talk not to me of fear!" said Juliet. And she went home and told her father she would marry Paris. If she had spoken out and told her father the truth . . . well, then this would have been a different story.

Lord Capulet was very much pleased to get his own way, and set about inviting his friends and getting the wedding feast ready. Every one stayed up all night, for there was a great deal to do, and very little time to do it in. Lord Capulet was anxious to get Juliet married, because he saw she was very unhappy. Of course she was really fretting about her husband Romeo, but her father thought she was grieving for the death of her cousin Tybalt, and he thought marriage would give her something else to think about.

Early in the morning the nurse came to call Juliet, and to dress her for her wedding; but she would not wake, and at last the nurse cried out suddenly:

"Alas! alas! help! help! my lady's dead. Oh, well-a-day that ever I was born!"

Lady Capulet came running in, and then Lord Capulet, and Lord Paris, the bridegroom. There lay Juliet cold and white and lifeless, and all their weeping could not wake her. So it was a burying that day instead of a marrying. Meantime Friar Laurence had sent a messenger to Mantua with a letter to Romeo telling him of all these things; and all would have been well, only the messenger was delayed, and could not go.

But ill news travels fast. Romeo's servant, who knew the secret of the marriage but not of Juliet's pretended death, heard of her funeral, and hurried to Mantua to tell Romeo how his young wife was dead and lying in the grave.

"Is it so!" cried Romeo, heart-broken. "Then I will lie by Juliet's side tonight."

And he bought himself a poison, and went straight back to Verona. He hastened to the tomb where Juliet was lying. It was not a grave, but a vault. He broke open the door, and was just going down the stone steps that led to the vault where all the dead Capulets lay, when he heard a voice behind him calling on him to stop.

It was the Count Paris, who was to have married Juliet that very day.

"How dare you come here and disturb the dead bodies of the Capulets, you vile Montagu!" cried Paris.

Poor Romeo, half mad with sorrow, yet tried to answer gently.

"You were told," said Paris, "that if you returned to Verona you must die."

"I must indeed," said Romeo. "I came here for nothing else. Good, gentle youth—leave me— Oh, go—before I do you any harm— I love you better than myself—go—leave me here—"

Then Paris said, "I defy you—and I arrest you as a felon." Then Romeo, in his anger and despair, drew his sword. They fought, and Paris was killed.

As Romeo's sword pierced him, Paris cried,

"Oh, I am slain! If thou be merciful, open the tomb, lay me with Juliet!"

And Romeo said, "In faith I will."

And he carried the dead man into the tomb and laid him by the dear Juliet's side. Then he kneeled by Juliet and spoke to her, and held her in his arms, and kissed her cold lips, believing that she was dead, while all the while she was coming nearer and nearer to the time of her awakening. Then he drank the poison, and died beside his sweetheart and wife.

Now came Friar Laurence when it was too late, and saw all that had happened—and then poor Juliet woke out of her sleep to find her husband and her friend both dead beside her.

The noise of the fight had brought other folks to the place too, and Friar Laurence hearing them ran away, and Juliet was left alone. She saw the cup that had held the poison, and knew how all had happened, and since no poison was left for

her, she drew Romeo's dagger and thrust it through her heart
—and so, falling with her head on her Romeo's breast, she
died. And here ends the story of these faithful and most unhappy lovers.

And when the old folks knew from Friar Laurence of all
that had befallen, they sorrowed exceedingly, and now, seeing
all the mischief their wicked quarrel had wrought, they repented them of it, and over the bodies of their dead children
they clasped hands at last, in friendship and forgiveness.

The Tempest

PROSPERO, the Duke of Milan, was a learned and studious man, who lived among his books, leaving the management of his dukedom to his brother Antonio, in whom indeed he had complete trust. But that trust was ill-rewarded, for Antonio wanted to wear the duke's crown himself, and, to gain his ends, would have killed his brother but for the love the people bore him. However, with the help of Prospero's great enemy, Alonso, King of Naples, he managed to get into his hands the dukedom with all its honor, power, and riches. For they took Prospero to sea, and when they were far away from land, forced him into a little boat with no tackle, mast, or sail. In their cruelty and hatred they put his little daughter, Miranda (not yet three years old), into the boat with him, and sailed away, leaving them to their fate.

But one among the courtiers with Antonio was true to his rightful master, Prospero. To save the duke from his enemies was impossible, but much could be done to remind him of a subject's love. So this worthy lord, whose name was Gonzalo, secretly placed in the boat some fresh water, provisions, and clothes, and what Prospero valued most of all, some of his precious books.

The boat was cast on an island, and Prospero and his little one landed in safety. Now this island was enchanted, and for years had lain under the spell of a fell witch, Sycorax, who had imprisoned in the trunks of trees all the good spirits she found there. She died shortly before Prospero was cast on those shores, but the spirits, of whom Ariel was the chief, still remained in their prisons.

Prospero was a great magician, for he had devoted himself almost entirely to the study of magic during the years in which he allowed his brother to manage the affairs of Milan. By his art he set free the imprisoned spirits, yet kept them obedient to his will, and they were more truly his subjects than his people in Milan had been. For he treated them kindly as long as they did his bidding, and he exercised his power over them wisely and well. One creature alone he found it necessary to treat with harshness: this was Caliban, the son of the wicked old witch, a hideous, deformed monster, horrible to look on, and vicious and brutal in all his habits.

When Miranda was grown up into a maiden, sweet and fair to see, it chanced that Antonio, and Alonso with Sebastian, his brother, and Ferdinand, his son, were at sea together with old Gonzalo, and their ship came near Prospero's island. Prospero, knowing they were there, raised by his art a great storm, so that even the sailors on board gave themselves up for lost; and first among them all Prince Ferdinand leaped into the sea, and his father thought in his grief he was drowned. But Ariel brought him safe ashore; and all the rest of the crew, although they were washed overboard, were landed unhurt in different parts of the island, and the good ship herself, which they all thought had been wrecked, lay at anchor in the harbor whither Ariel had brought her. Such wonders could Prospero and his spirits perform.

While yet the tempest was raging, Prospero showed his daughter the brave ship laboring in the trough of the sea, and told her that it was filled with living human beings like themselves. She, in pity of their lives, prayed him who had raised this storm to quell it. Then her father bade her to have no fear, for he intended to save every one of them.

Then, for the first time, he told her the story of his life and hers, and that he had caused this storm to rise in order that his enemies, Antonio and Alonso, who were on board, might be delivered into his hands.

When he had made an end of his story he charmed her into sleep, for Ariel was at hand, and he had work for him to do.

Ariel, who longed for his complete freedom, grumbled to be kept in drudgery, but on being threateningly reminded of all the sufferings he had undergone when Sycorax ruled in the land, and of the debt of gratitude he owed to the master who had made those sufferings to end, he ceased to complain, and promised faithfully to do whatever Prospero might command.

"Do so," said Prospero, "and in two days I will discharge thee."

Then he bade Ariel take the form of a water nymph and sent him in search of the young prince. And Ariel, invisible to Ferdinand, hovered near him, singing the while:

> *"Come unto these yellow sands,*
> *And then take hands:*
> *Court'sied when you have, and kiss'd,—*
> *The wild waves whist,—*
> *Foot it featly here and there;*
> *And, sweet sprites, the burden bear."*

And Ferdinand followed the magic singing, as the song changed to a solemn air, and the words brought grief to his heart, and tears to his eyes, for thus they ran:

> *"Full fathom five thy father lies;*
> *Of his bones are coral made:*
> *Those are pearls that were his eyes:*
> *Nothing of him that doth fade,*

Prospero, with his magic, raises a great storm

But doth suffer a sea-change
Into something rich and strange.
Sea-nymphs hourly ring his knell.
Hark! now I hear them,—ding dong bell."

And so singing, Ariel led the spell-bound prince into the presence of Prospero and Miranda. Then, behold! all happened as Prospero desired. For Miranda, who had never, since she could first remember, seen any human being save her father, looked on the youthful prince with reverence in her eyes, and love in her secret heart.

"I might call him," she said, "a thing divine, for nothing natural I ever saw so noble!"

And Ferdinand, beholding her beauty with wonder and delight, exclaimed:

"Most sure, the goddess on whom these airs attend!"

Nor did he attempt to hide the passion which she inspired in him, for scarcely had they exchanged half a dozen sentences, before he vowed to make her his queen if she were willing. But Prospero, though secretly delighted, pretended wrath.

"You come here as a spy," he said to Ferdinand. "I will manacle your neck and feet together, and you shall feed on fresh water mussels, withered roots and husk, and have sea-water to drink. Follow."

"No," said Ferdinand, and drew his sword. But on the instant Prospero charmed him so that he stood there like a statue, still as stone; and Miranda in terror prayed her father to have mercy on her lover. But he harshly refused her, and made Ferdinand follow him to his cell. There he set the prince to work, making him remove thousands of heavy logs of timber and pile them up; and Ferdinand patiently obeyed, and thought his toil all too well repaid by the sympathy of the sweet Miranda.

She in very pity would have helped him in his hard work, but he would not let her, yet he could not keep from her the secret of his love, and she, hearing it, rejoiced and promised to be his wife.

Then Prospero released him from his servitude, and glad at heart, he gave his consent to their marriage.

"Take her," he said, "she is thine own."

In the meantime, Antonio and Sebastian in another part of the island were plotting the murder of Alonso, the King of Naples, for Ferdinand being dead, as they thought, Sebastian would succeed to the throne on Alonso's death. And they would have carried out their wicked purpose while their victim was asleep, but that Ariel woke him in good time.

Many tricks did Ariel play them. Once he set a banquet before them, and just as they were going to fall to, he appeared to them amid thunder and lightning in the form of a harpy, and immediately the banquet disappeared. Then Ariel upbraided them with their sins and vanished too.

Prospero by his enchantments drew them all to the grove without his cell, where they waited, trembling and afraid, and now at last bitterly repenting them of their sins.

Prospero determined to make one last use of his magic power, "and then," said he, "I'll break my staff and deeper than did ever plummet sound I'll drown my book."

So he made heavenly music to sound in the air, and appeared to them in his proper shape as the Duke of Milan. Because they repented, he forgave them and told them the story of his life since they had cruelly committed him and his baby daughter to the mercy of wind and waves. Alonso, who seemed sorriest of them all for his past crimes, lamented the loss of his heir. But Prospero drew back a curtain and showed them Ferdinand and Miranda playing at chess. Great was Alonso's joy to greet his loved son again, and when he heard that the fair maid with whom Ferdinand was playing was Prospero's daughter, and that the young folks had plighted their troth, he said:

"Give me your hands, let grief and sorrow still embrace his heart that doth not wish you joy."

So all ended happily. The ship was safe in the harbor, and next day they all set sail for Naples, where Ferdinand and

Miranda were to be married. Ariel gave them calm seas and auspicious gales; and many were the rejoicings at the wedding.

Then Prospero, after many years of absence, went back to his own dukedom, where he was welcomed with great joy by his faithful subjects. He practiced the arts of magic no more, but his life was happy, and not only because he had found his own again, but chiefly because, when his bitterest foes who had done him deadly wrong lay at his mercy, he took no vengeance on them, but nobly forgave them.

As for Ariel, Prospero made him free as air, so that he could wander where he would, and sing with a light heart his sweet song.

> *"Where the bee sucks, there suck I:*
> *In a cowslip's bell I lie;*
> *There I couch when owls do cry.*
> *On the bat's back I do fly*
> *After summer merrily:*
> *Merrily, merrily shall I live now*
> *Under the blossom that hangs on the bough."*

A
Midsummer Night's
Dream

HERMIA and Lysander were lovers; but Hermia's father wished her to marry another man, named Demetrius.

Now in Athens, where they lived, there was a wicked law, by which any girl who refused to marry according to her father's wishes, might be put to death. Hermia's father was so angry with her for refusing to do as he wished, that he actually brought her before the Duke of Athens to ask that she might be killed, if she still refused to obey him. The Duke gave her four days to think about it, and, at the end of that time, if she still refused to marry Demetrius, she would have to die.

Lysander of course was nearly mad with grief, and the best thing to do seemed to him for Hermia to run away to his aunt's house at a place beyond the reach of that cruel law; and there he would come to her and marry her. But before she started, she told her friend, Helena, what she was going to do.

Helena had been Demetrius' sweetheart long before his marriage with Hermia had been thought of, and being very silly, like all jealous people, she could not see that it was not poor Hermia's fault that Demetrius wished to marry her instead of his own lady, Helena. She knew that if she told Demetrius that Hermia was going, as she was, to the wood outside Athens, he would follow her, "and I can follow him, and at least I shall see him," she said to herself. So she went to him, and betrayed her friend's secret.

Now this wood where Lysander was to meet Hermia, and where the other two had decided to follow them, was full of fairies, as most woods are, if one only had the eyes to see them, and in this wood on this night were the King and Queen of the fairies, Oberon and Titania. Now fairies are very wise people, but now and then they can be quite as foolish as mortal folk. Oberon and Titania, who might have been as happy as the days were long, had thrown away all their joy in a foolish quarrel. They never met without saying disagreeable things to each other, and scolded each other so dreadfully that all their little fairy followers, for fear, would creep into acorn cups and hide.

So, instead of keeping one happy Court and dancing all night through in the moonlight, as is fairies' use, the King with his attendants wandered through one part of the wood, while the Queen with hers kept state in another. And the cause of all this trouble was a little Indian boy whom Titania had taken to be one of her followers. Oberon wanted the child to follow him and be one of his fairy knights; but the Queen would not give him up.

On this night, in a glossy moonlight glade, the King and Queen of the fairies met.

"Ill met by moonlight, proud Titania," said the King.

"What! jealous, Oberon?" answered the Queen. "You spoil everything with your quarreling. Come, fairies, let us leave him. I am not friends with him now."

"It rests with you to make up the quarrel," said the King. "Give me that little Indian boy, and I will again be your humble servant and suitor."

"Set your mind at rest," said the Queen. "Your whole fairy kingdom buys not that boy from me. Come, fairies."

And she and her train rode off down the moonbeams.

"Well, go your ways," said Oberon. "But I'll be even with you before you leave this wood."

Then Oberon called his favorite fairy, Puck. Puck was the spirit of mischief. He used to slip into the dairies and take the cream away, and get into the churn so that the butter would not come, and turn the beer sour, and lead people out of their way on dark nights and then laugh at them, and tumble people's stools from under them when they were going to sit down, and upset their hot ale over their chins when they were going to drink.

"Now," said Oberon to this little sprite, "fetch me the flower called Love-in-idleness. The juice of that little purple flower laid on the eyes of those who sleep will make them when they wake to love the first thing they see. I will put some of the juice of that flower on my Titania's eyes, and when she wakes, she will love the first thing she sees, were it lion, bear, or wolf, or bull, or meddling monkey, or a busy ape."

While Puck was gone, Demetrius passed through the glade followed by poor Helena, and still she told him how she loved him and reminded him of all his promises, and still he told her that he did not and could not love her, and that his promises were nothing. Oberon was sorry for poor Helena, and when Puck returned with the flower, he bade him follow Demetrius and put some of the juice on his eyes, so that he might love Helena when he woke and looked on her, as much as she loved him. So Puck set off, and wandering through the wood found, not Demetrius, but Lysander, on whose eyes he put the juice; but when Lysander woke, he saw not his own Hermia, but Helena, who was walking through the wood looking for the cruel Demetrius; and directly he saw her he loved her and left his own lady, under the spell of the crimson flower.

When Hermia woke she found Lysander gone, and wandered about the wood trying to find him. Puck went back and told Oberon what he had done, and Oberon soon found that he had made a mistake, and set about looking for Demetrius, and having found him, put some of the juice on his eyes. And the first thing Demetrius saw when he woke was also Helena. So now Demetrius and Lysander were both following her through the wood, and it was Hermia's turn to follow her lover as Helena had done before. The end of it was that Helena and Hermia began to quarrel, and Demetrius and Lysander went off to fight. Oberon was very sorry to see his kind scheme to help these lovers turn out so badly. So he said to Puck:

"These two young men are going to fight. You must overhang the night with drooping fog, and lead them so astray, that one will never find the other. When they are tired out, they will fall asleep. Then drop this other herb on Lysander's eyes. That will give him his old sight and his old love. Then each man will have the lady who loves him, and they will all think that this has been only a Midsummer Night's Dream. Then when this is done all will be well with them."

So Puck went and did as he was told, and when the two

had fallen asleep without meeting each other, Puck poured
the juice on Lysander's eyes, and said:

> *"When thou wak'st*
> *Thou tak'st*
> *True delight*
> *In the sight*
> *Of thy former lady's eye:*
> *Jack shall have Jill;*
> *Nought shall go ill;*
> *The man shall have his mare again,*
> *And all shall be well."*

Meanwhile Oberon found Titania asleep on a bank where
grew wild thyme, oxlips, and violets, and woodbine, musk
roses and eglantine. There Titania always slept a part of the
night, wrapped in the enameled skin of a snake. Oberon
stooped over her and laid the juice on her eyes, saying:

> *"What thou seest when thou wake,*
> *Do it for thy true love take."*

Now, it happened that when Titania woke the first thing
she saw was a stupid clown, one of a party of players who had
come out into the wood to rehearse their play. This clown
had met with Puck, who had clapped an ass's head on his
shoulders so that it looked as if it grew there. Directly Titania

Titania awakens and falls in love with the clown

woke and saw this dreadful monster, she said, "What angel is this? Are you as wise as you are beautiful?"

"If I am wise enough to find my way out of this wood, that's enough for me," said the foolish clown.

"Do not desire to go out of the wood," said Titania. The spell of the love-juice was on her, and to her the clown seemed the most beautiful and delightful creature on all the earth. "I love you," she went on. "Come with me, and I will give you fairies to attend on you."

So she called four fairies, whose names were Peaseblossom, Cobweb, Moth, and Mustardseed.

"You must attend this gentleman," said the Queen. "Feed him with apricots, and dewberries, purple grapes, green figs, and mulberries. Steal honey-bags for him from the humble-bees, and with the wings of painted butterflies fan the moon-beams from his sleeping eyes."

"I will," said one of the fairies, and all the others said, "I will."

"Now, sit down with me," said the Queen to the clown, "and let me stroke your dear cheeks, and stick musk roses in your smooth, sleek head, and kiss your fair large ears, my gentle joy."

"Where's Peaseblossom?" asked the clown with the ass's

head. He did not care much about the Queen's affection, but he was very proud of having fairies to wait on him.

"Ready," said Peaseblossom.

"Scratch my head, Peaseblossom," said the clown. "Where's Cobweb?"

"Ready," said Cobweb.

"Kill me," said the clown, "the red humble-bee on the top of the thistle yonder, and bring me the honey-bag. Where's Mustardseed?"

"Ready," said Mustardseed.

"Oh, I want nothing," said the clown. "Only just help Cobweb to scratch. I must go to the barber's, for methinks I am marvelous hairy about the face."

"Would you like anything to eat?" said the fairy Queen.

"I should like some good dry oats," said the clown—for his donkey's head made him desire donkey's food—"and some hay to follow."

"Shall some of my fairies fetch you new nuts from the squirrel's house?" asked the Queen.

"I'd rather have a handful or two of good dried peas," said the clown. "But please don't let any of your people disturb me, I am going to sleep."

Then said the Queen, "And I will wind thee in my arms."

And so when Oberon came along he found his beautiful

Queen lavishing kisses and endearments on a clown with a donkey's head. And before he released her from the enchantment, he persuaded her to give him the little Indian boy he so much desired to have. Then he took pity on her, and threw some juice of the disenchanting flower on her pretty eyes; and then in a moment she saw plainly the donkey-headed clown she had been loving, and knew how foolish she had been.

Oberon took off the ass's head from the clown, and left him to finish his sleep with his own silly head lying on the thyme and violets.

Thus all was made plain and straight again. Oberon and Titania loved each other more than ever. Demetrius thought of no one but Helena, and Helena had never had any thought of anyone but Demetrius. As for Hermia and Lysander, they were as loving a couple as you could meet in a day's march, even through a fairy-wood. So the four mortal lovers went back to Athens and were married; and the fairy King and Queen live happily together in that very wood at this very day.

Cordelia is banished by her father, King Lear

King Lear

KING LEAR was old and tired. He was aweary of the business of his kingdom, and wished only to end his days quietly near his three daughters, whom he loved dearly. Two of his daughters were married to the Dukes of Albany and Cornwall; and the Duke of Burgundy and the King of France were both staying at Lear's Court as suitors for the hand of Cordelia, his youngest daughter.

Lear called his three daughters together, and told them that he proposed to divide his kingdom between them. "But first," said he, "I should like to know how much you love me."

Goneril, who was really a very wicked woman, and did not love her father at all, said she loved him more than words could say; she loved him dearer than eyesight, space or liberty, more than life, grace, health, beauty, and honor.

"If you love me as much as this," said the King, "I give you a third part of my kingdom. And how much does Regan love me?"

"I love you as much as my sister and more," professed Regan, "since I care for nothing but my father's love."

Lear was very much pleased with Regan's professions, and gave her another third part of his fair kingdom. Then he turned to his youngest daughter, Cordelia. "Now, our joy, though last not least," he said, "the best part of my kingdom have I kept for you. What can you say?"

"Nothing, my lord," answered Cordelia.

"Nothing?"

"Nothing," said Cordelia.

"Nothing can come of nothing. Speak again," said the King.

And Cordelia answered, "I love your Majesty according to my duty—no more, no less."

And this she said, because she knew her sisters' wicked hearts, and was disgusted with the way in which they professed unbounded and impossible love, when really they had not even a right sense of duty to their old father.

"I am your daughter," she went on, "and you have brought me up and loved me, and I return you those duties back as are right fit, obey you, love you, and most honor you."

Lear, who loved Cordelia best, had wished her to make more extravagant professions of love than her sisters; and what seemed to him her coldness so angered him that he bade her begone from his sight. "Go," he said, "be for ever a stranger to my heart and me."

The Earl of Kent, one of Lear's favorite courtiers and captains, tried to say a word for Cordelia's sake, but Lear would not listen. He divided the remaining part of his kingdom between Goneril and Regan, who had pleased him with their foolish flattery, and told them that he should only keep a hundred knights at arms for his following, and would live with his daughters by turns.

When the Duke of Burgundy knew that Cordelia would have no share of the kingdom, he gave up his courtship of her. But the King of France was wiser, and said to her, "Fairest Cordelia, thou art most rich, being poor—most choice, forsaken; and most loved, despised. Thee and thy virtues here I seize upon. Thy dowerless daughter, King, is Queen of us— of ours, and our fair France."

"Take her, take her," said the King; "for I have no such daughter, and will never see that face of hers again."

So Cordelia became Queen of France, and the Earl of Kent, for having ventured to take her part, was banished from the King's Court and from the kingdom. The King now went to stay with his daughter Goneril, and very soon began to find out how much fair words were worth. She had got everything from her father that he had to give, and she began to grudge even the hundred knights that he had reserved for himself. She frowned at him whenever she met him; she herself was harsh and undutiful to him, and her servants treated him with neglect, and either refused to obey his orders or pretended that they did not hear them.

Now the Earl of Kent, when he was banished, made as though he would go into another country, but instead he came back in the disguise of a serving-man and took service with the King, who never suspected him to be that Earl of Kent whom he himself had banished. The very same day that Lear engaged him as his servant, Goneril's steward insulted the King, and the Earl of Kent showed his respect for the King's Majesty by tripping up the caitiff into the gutter. The King had now two friends—the Earl of Kent, whom he only knew as his servant, and his Fool, who was faithful to him although he had given away his kingdom. Goneril was not contented with letting her father suffer insults at the hands of her servants. She told him plainly that his train of one hundred knights only served to fill her Court with riot and feasting; and so she begged him to dismiss them, and only keep a few old men about him such as himself.

"My train are men who know all parts of duty," said Lear. "Saddle my horses, call my train together. Goneril, I will not trouble you further—yet I have left another daughter."

And he cursed his daughter, Goneril, praying that she might never have a child, or that if she had, it might treat her as cruelly as she had treated him. And his horses being saddled, he set out with his followers for the castle of Regan, his other daughter. Lear sent on his servant Caius, who was really the Earl of Kent, with letters to his daughter to say he was coming. But Caius fell in with a messenger of Goneril—in fact that very steward whom he had tripped into the gutter—and beat him soundly for the mischief-maker that he was; and Regan, when she heard it, put Caius in the stocks, not respecting him as a messenger coming from her father. And she who had formerly outdone her sister in professions of attachment to the King, now seemed to outdo her in undutiful conduct, saying that fifty knights were too many to wait on him, that five-and-twenty were enough, and Goneril (who had hurried thither to prevent Regan showing any kindness to the old King) said five-and-twenty were too many, or even ten, or even five, since her servants could wait on him.

"What need one?" said Regan.

Then when Lear saw that what they really wanted was to drive him away from them, he cursed them both and left them. It was a wild and stormy night, yet those cruel daughters did not care what became of their father in the cold and the rain, but they shut the castle doors and went in out of the storm. All night he wandered about the heath half mad with misery, and with no companion but the poor Fool. But presently his servant Caius, the good Earl of Kent, met him, and at last persuaded him to lie down in a wretched little hovel which stood upon the heath. At daybreak the Earl of Kent removed his royal master to Dover, where his old friends were, and then hurried to the Court of France and told Cordelia what had happened.

Her husband gave her an army to go to the assistance of her father, and with it she landed at Dover. Here she found poor King Lear, now quite mad, wandering about the fields, singing aloud to himself and wearing a crown of nettles and weeds. They brought him back and fed and clothed him, and the doctors gave him such medicines as they thought might bring him back to his right mind, and by-and-by he woke better, but still not quite himself. Then Cordelia came to him and kissed him, to make up, as she said, for the cruelty of her sisters. At first he hardly knew her.

"Pray do not mock me," he said. "I am a very foolish, fond old man, four-score and upward, and to deal plainly, I fear I am not in my perfect mind. I think I should know you, though I do not know these garments, nor do I know where I lodged last night. Do not laugh at me, though, as I am a man, I think this lady must be my daughter, Cordelia."

"And so I am—I am," cried Cordelia. "Come with me."

"You must bear with me," said Lear; "forget and forgive. I am old and foolish."

And now he knew at last which of his children it was that had loved him best, and who was worthy of his love; and from that time they were not parted.

Goneril and Regan joined their armies to fight Cordelia's army, and were successful: and Cordelia and her father were thrown into prison. Then Goneril's husband, the Duke of Albany, who was a good man, and had not known how wicked his wife was, heard the truth of the whole story; and when Goneril found that her husband knew her for the wicked woman she was, she killed herself, having a little time before given a deadly poison to her sister, Regan, out of a spirit of jealousy.

But they had arranged that Cordelia should be hanged in prison, and though the Duke of Albany sent messengers at once, it was too late. The old King came staggering into the tent of the Duke of Albany, carrying the body of his dear daughter Cordelia in his arms.

"Oh, she is gone forever," he said. "I know when one is dead, and when one lives. She's dead as earth."

They crowded round in horror.

"Oh, if she lives," said the King, "it is a chance that does redeem all sorrows that ever I have felt."

The Earl of Kent spoke a word to him, but Lear was too mad to listen.

"A plague upon you murderous traitors all! I might have saved her. Now she is gone forever. Cordelia, Cordelia, stay a little. Her voice was ever low, gentle, and soft—an excellent thing in woman. I killed the slave that was hanging thee."

" 'Tis true, my lords, he did," said one of the officers from the castle.

"Oh, thou wilt come no more," cried the poor old man. "Do you see this? Look on her—look, her lips. Look there, look there."

And with that he fell with her still in his arms, and died.

And this was the end of Lear and Cordelia.

Cymbeline

CYMBELINE was the King of Britain. He had three children. The two sons were stolen away from him when they were quite little children, and he was left with only one daughter, Imogen. The King married a second time, and brought up Leonatus, the son of a dead friend, as Imogen's playfellow; and when Leonatus was old enough, Imogen secretly married him. This made the King and Queen very angry, and the King, to punish Leonatus, banished him from Britain.

Poor Imogen was nearly heart-broken at parting from Leonatus, and he was not less unhappy. For they were not only lovers and husband and wife, but they had been friends and comrades ever since they were quite little children. With many tears and kisses they said "Good-bye." They promised never to forget each other, and that they would never care for any one else as long as they lived.

"This diamond was my mother's love," said Imogen; "take it, my heart, and keep it as long as you love me."

"Sweetest, fairest," answered Leonatus, "wear this bracelet for my sake."

"Ah?" cried Imogen, weeping, "when shall we meet again?"

And while they were still in each other's arms, the King came in, and Leonatus had to leave without more farewell.

When he was come to Rome, where he had gone to stay with an old friend of his father's, he spent his days still in thinking of his dear Imogen, and his nights in dreaming of her. One day at a feast some Italian and French noblemen were talking of their sweethearts, and swearing that they were the most faithful and honorable and beautiful ladies in the world. And a Frenchman reminded Leonatus how he had said many times that his wife Imogen was more fair, wise, and constant than any of the rest of the ladies in France.

"I say so still," said Leonatus.

"She is not so good but that she would deceive," said Iachimo, one of the Italian nobles.

"She never would deceive," said Leonatus.

"I wager," said Iachimo, "that, if I go to Britain, I can persuade your wife to do whatever I wish, even if it should be against your wishes."

"That you will never do," said Leonatus. "I wager this ring upon my finger," which was the very ring Imogen had given him at parting, "that my wife will keep all her vows to me, and that you will never persuade her to do otherwise."

So Iachimo wagered half his estate against the ring on Leonatus' finger, and started forthwith to Britain with a letter of introduction to Leonatus' wife. When he reached there he was received with all kindness; but he was still determined to win his wager.

He told Imogen that her husband thought no more of her, and went on to tell many cruel lies about him. Imogen listened at first, but presently perceived what a wicked person Iachimo was, and ordered him to leave her. Then he said:

"Pardon me, fair lady, all that I have said is untrue. I only told you this to see whether you would believe me, or whether you were as much to be trusted as your husband thinks. Will you forgive me?"

"I forgive you freely," said Imogen.

"Then," went on Iachimo, "perhaps you will prove it by taking charge of a trunk, containing a number of jewels which your husband and I and some other gentlemen have bought as a present for the Emperor of Rome."

"I will indeed," said Imogen, "do anything for my husband and a friend of my husband's. Have the jewels sent into my room, and I will take care of them."

"It is only for one night," said Iachimo, "for I leave Britain again tomorrow."

So the trunk was carried into Imogen's room, and that night she went to bed and to sleep. When she was fast asleep, the lid of the trunk opened and a man got out. It was Iachimo. The story about the jewels was as untrue as the rest of the things he had said. He had only wished to get into her room to win his wicked wager. He looked about him and noticed the furniture, and then crept to the side of the bed where Imogen was asleep and took from her arm the gold bracelet which had been the parting gift of her husband. Then he crept back to the trunk, and next morning sailed for Rome.

When he met Leonatus, he said:

"I have been to Britain and I have won the wager, for your wife no longer thinks about you. She stayed talking with me all one night in her room, which is hung with tapestry and has a carved chimney-piece, and silver andirons in the shape of two winking cupids."

"I do not believe she has forgotten me; I do not believe she stayed talking with you in her room. You have heard her room described by the servants."

"Ah!" said Iachimo, "but she gave me this bracelet. She took it from her arm. I see her yet. Her pretty action did outsell her gift, and yet enriched it too. She gave it me, and said she prized it once."

"Take the ring," cried Leonatus, "you have won, and you might have won my life as well, for I care nothing for it now I know my lady has forgotten me."

And mad with anger, he wrote letters to Britain to his old servant, Pisanio, ordering him to take Imogen to Milford Haven, and murder her, because she had forgotten him and given away his gift. At the same time he wrote to Imogen herself, telling her to go with Pisanio, his old servant, to Milford Haven, and that he, her husband, would be there to meet her.

Now when Pisanio got this letter he was too good to carry out its orders, and too wise to let them alone altogether. So he gave Imogen the letter from her husband, and started with her for Milford Haven. Before he left, the wicked Queen gave him a drink which, she said, would be useful in sickness. She hoped he would give it to Imogen, and that Imogen would die, and then the wicked Queen's son could be King. For the Queen thought this drink was a poison, but really and truly it was only a sleeping-draught.

When Pisanio and Imogen came near to Milford Haven, he told her what was really in the letter he had had from her husband.

"I must go on to Rome, and see him myself," said Imogen.

And then Pisanio helped her to dress in boy's clothes, and sent her on her way, and went back to the Court. Before he went, he gave her the drink he had had from the Queen.

Imogen went on, getting more and more tired, and at last came to a cave. Some one seemed to live there, but no one was in just then. So she went in, and as she was almost dying of hunger, she took some food she saw there, and had just done so, when an old man and two boys came into the cave. She was very much frightened when she saw them, for she thought that they would be angry with her for taking their food, though she had meant to leave money for it on the table. But to her surprise they welcomed her kindly. She looked very pretty in her boy's clothes, and her face was good, as well as pretty.

"You shall be our brother," said both the boys; and so she stayed with them, and helped to cook the food, and make things comfortable. But one day when the old man, whose name was Bellarius, was out hunting with the two boys, Imogen felt ill, and thought she would try the medicine Pisanio had given her. So she took it, and at once became like a dead creature, so that when Bellarius and the boys came back from hunting, they thought she was dead, and with many tears and funeral songs, they carried her away and laid her in the wood, covered with flowers.

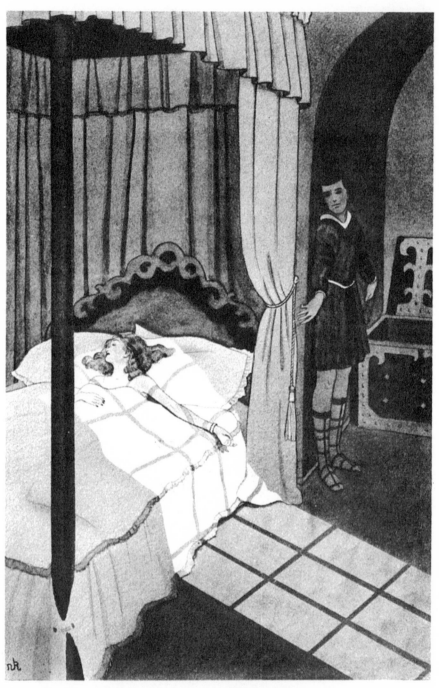

Iachimo: "O sleep! thou ape of death, lie dull upon her

They sang sweet songs to her, and strewed flowers on her, pale primroses, and the azure harebell, and eglantine, and furred moss, and went away sorrowful. No sooner had they gone than Imogen awoke, and not knowing how she came there, nor where she was, went wandering through the wood.

Now while Imogen had been living in the cave, the Romans had decided to attack Britain, and their army had come over, and with them Leonatus, who had grown sorry for his wickedness against Imogen, so had come back, not to fight with the Romans against Britain, but with the Britons against Rome. So as Imogen wandered alone, she met with Lucius, the Roman General, and took service with him as his page.

When the battle was fought between the Romans and Britons, Bellarius and his two boys fought for their own country, and Leonatus, disguised as a British peasant, fought beside them. The Romans had taken Cymbeline prisoner, and old Bellarius, with his sons and Leonatus, bravely rescued the King. Then the Britons won the battle, and among the prisoners brought before the King were Lucius, with Imogen, Iachimo, and Leonatus, who had put on the uniform of a Roman soldier. He was tired of his life since he had cruelly ordered his wife to be killed, and he hoped that, as a Roman soldier, he would be put to death.

When they were brought before the King, Lucius spoke out:

"A Roman with a Roman's heart can suffer," he said. "If I must die, so be it. This one thing only will I entreat. My boy, a Briton born, let him be ransomed. Never master had a page so kind, so duteous, diligent, true. He has done no Briton harm, though he has served a Roman. Save him, sir."

Then Cymbeline looked on the page, who was his own daughter, Imogen, in disguise, and though he did not recognize her, he felt such a kindness that he not only spared the boy's life, but he said:

"He shall have any boon he likes to ask of me, even though he ask a prisoner, the noblest taken."

Then Imogen said, "The boon I ask is that this gentleman shall say from whom he got the ring he has on his finger," and she pointed to Iachimo.

"Speak," said Cymbeline, "how did you get that diamond?"

Then Iachimo told the whole truth of his villainy. At this, Leonatus was unable to contain himself, and casting aside all thought of disguise, he came forward, cursing himself for his folly in having believed Iachimo's lying story, and calling again and again on his wife whom he believed dead.

"Oh, Imogen, my love, my life!" he cried. "Oh, Imogen!"

Then Imogen, forgetting she was disguised, cried out, "Peace, my lord—here, here!"

Leonatus turned to strike the forward page who thus interfered in his great trouble, and then he saw that it was his wife, Imogen, and they fell into each other's arms.

The King was so glad to see his dear daughter again, and so grateful to the man who had rescued him (whom he now found to be Leonatus), that he gave his blessing on their marriage, and then he turned to Bellarius, and the two boys. Now Bellarius spoke:

"I am your old servant, Bellarius. You accused me of treason when I had only been loyal to you, and to be doubted, made me disloyal. So I stole your two sons, and see,—they are here!" And he brought forward the two boys, who had sworn to be brothers to Imogen when they thought she was a boy like themselves.

The wicked Queen was dead of some of her own poisons, and the King, with his three children about him, lived to a happy old age.

So the wicked were punished, and the good and true lived happy ever after. So may the wicked suffer, and honest folk prosper till the world's end.

Petruchio: "But for my Bonny Kate, she must with me!"

The Taming of the Shrew

THERE lived in Padua a gentleman named Baptista, who had two fair daughters. The eldest, Katharine, was so very cross and ill-tempered, and unmannerly, that no one ever dreamed of marrying her, while her sister, Bianca, was so sweet and pretty, and pleasant-spoken, that more than one suitor asked her father for her hand. But Baptista said the elder daughter must marry first.

So Bianca's suitors decided among themselves to try and get some one to marry Katharine—and then the father could at least be got to listen to their suit for Bianca.

A gentleman from Verona, named Petruchio, was the one they thought of, and, half in jest, they asked him if he would marry Katharine, the disagreeable scold. Much to their surprise he said yes, that was just the sort of wife for him, and if Katharine were handsome and rich, he himself would undertake soon to make her good-tempered.

Petruchio started by asking Baptista's permission to pay court to his gentle daughter Katharine—and Baptista was obliged to own that she was anything but gentle. And just then her music master rushed in, complaining that the naughty girl had broken her lute over his head, because he told her she was not playing correctly.

"Never mind," said Petruchio, "I love her better than ever, and long to have some chat with her."

When Katharine came, he said, "Good-morrow, Kate—for that, I hear, is your name."

"You've only heard half," said Katharine, rudely.

"Oh, no," said Petruchio, "they call you plain Kate, and bonny Kate, and sometimes Kate the shrew, and so, hearing your mildness praised in every town, and your beauty too, I ask you for my wife."

"Your wife!" cried Kate. "Never!" She said some extremely disagreeable things to him, and, I am sorry to say, ended by boxing his ears.

"If you do that again, I'll cuff you," he said quietly; and still protested, with many compliments, that he would marry none but her.

When Baptista came back, he asked at once, "How speed you with my daughter?"

"How should I speed but well," replied Petruchio, "how, but well?"

"How now, daughter Katharine?" the father went on.

"I don't think," said Katharine, angrily, "you are acting a father's part in wishing me to marry this mad-cap ruffian."

"Ah!" said Petruchio, "you and all the world would talk amiss of her. You should see how kind she is to me when we are alone. In short, I will go off to Venice to buy fine things for our wedding—for—kiss me, Kate! we will be married on Sunday."

And with that, Katharine flounced out of the room by one door in a violent temper, and he, laughing, went out by the other. But whether she fell in love with Petruchio, or whether she was only glad to meet a man who was not afraid of her, or whether she was flattered that in spite of her rough words and spiteful usage, he still desired her for his wife—she did indeed marry him on Sunday, as he had sworn she should.

To vex and humble Katharine's naughty, proud spirit, he was late at the wedding, and when he came, came wearing such shabby clothes that she was ashamed to be seen with him. His servant was dressed in the same shabby way, and the horses they rode were the sport of everyone they passed.

And, after the marriage, when should have been the wedding breakfast, Petruchio carried his wife away, not allowing her to eat or drink—saying that she was his now, and he could do as he liked with her.

And his manner was so violent, and he behaved all through

his wedding in so mad and dreadful a manner, that Katharine trembled and went with him. He mounted her on a stumbling, lean, old horse, and they journeyed by rough muddy ways to Petruchio's house, he scolding and snarling all the way.

She was terribly tired when she reached her new home, but Petruchio was determined that she should neither eat nor sleep that night, for he had made up his mind to teach his bad-tempered wife a lesson she would never forget.

So he welcomed her kindly to his house, but when supper was served he found fault with everything—the meat was burnt, he said, and ill-served, and he loved her far too much to let her eat anything but the best. At last Katharine, tired out with her journey, went supperless to bed. Then her husband, still telling her how he loved her, and how anxious he was that she should sleep well, pulled her bed to pieces, throwing pillows and bedclothes on the floor, so that she could not go to bed at all, and still kept growling and scolding at the servants so that Kate might see how unbeautiful a thing ill-temper was.

The next day, too, Katharine's food was all found fault with, and caught away before she could touch a mouthful, and she was sick and giddy for want of sleep. Then she said to one of the servants:

"I pray thee go and get me some repast. I care not what."

"What say you to a neat's foot?" said the servant.

Katharine said "Yes," eagerly; but the servant, who was in his master's secret, said he feared it was not good for hasty-tempered people. Would she like tripe?

"Bring it to me," said Katharine.

"I don't think *that* is good for hasty-tempered people," said the servant. "What do you say to a dish of beef and mustard?"

"I love it," said Kate.

"But mustard is too hot."

"Why, then, the beef, and let the mustard go," cried Katharine, who was getting hungrier and hungrier.

"No," said the servant, "you must have the mustard, or you get no beef from me."

"Then," cried Katharine, losing patience, "let it be both, or one, or anything thou wilt."

"Why, then," said the servant, "the mustard without the beef!"

Then Katharine saw he was making fun of her, and boxed *his* ears.

Just then Petruchio brought her some food—but she had scarcely begun to satisfy her hunger, before he called for the tailor to bring her new clothes, and the table was cleared, leaving her still hungry. Katharine was pleased with the pretty new dress and cap that the tailor had made for her, but Petruchio found fault with everything, flung the cap and gown on the floor, vowing his dear wife should not wear any such foolish things.

"I will have them," cried Katharine. "All gentlewomen wear such caps as these—"

"When you are gentle you shall have one too," he answered, "and not till then." When he had driven away the tailor with angry words—but privately asking his friend to see him paid—Petruchio said:

"Come, Kate, let's go to your father's, shabby as we are, for, as the sun breaks through the darkest clouds, so honor peereth in the meanest habit. It is about seven o'clock now. We shall easily get there by dinner-time."

"It's nearly two," said Kate, but civilly enough, for she had grown to see that she could not bully her husband, as she had done her father and her sister; "it's nearly two, and it will be supper-time before we get there."

"It shall be seven," said Petruchio, obstinately, "before I start. Why, whatever I say or do, or think, you do nothing but contradict. I won't go today, and before I do go, it shall be what o'clock I say it is."

At last they started for her father's house. "Look at the moon," said he.

"It's the sun," said Katharine, and indeed it was.

"I say it is the moon. Contradicting again! It shall be sun or moon, or whatever I choose, or I won't take you to your father's."

Then Katharine gave in, once and for all. "What you will have it named," she said, "it is, and so it shall be so for Katharine." And so it was, for from that moment Katharine felt that she had met her master, and never again showed her naughty tempers to him, or anyone else.

So they journeyed on to Baptista's house, and arriving there, they found all folks keeping Bianca's wedding feast, and that of another newly-married couple, Hortensio and his wife. They were made welcome, and sat down to the feast, and all was merry, save that Hortensio's wife, seeing Katharine subdued to her husband, thought she could safely say many disagreeable things, that in the old days, when Katharine was free and forward, she would not have dared to say. But Katharine answered with such spirit and such moderation, that she turned the laugh against the new bride.

After dinner, when the ladies were retired, Baptista joined in a laugh against Petruchio, saying:

"Now in good sadness, son Petruchio, I fear you have got the veriest shrew of all."

"You are wrong," said Petruchio; "let me prove it to you. Each of us shall send a message to his wife, desiring her to come to him, and the one whose wife comes most readily shall win a wager which he will agree on."

The others said yes readily enough, for each thought his own wife the most dutiful, and each thought he was quite sure to win the wager.

They proposed a wager of twenty crowns.

"Twenty crowns," said Petruchio, "I'll venture so much on my hawk or hound, but twenty times as much upon my wife."

"A hundred then," cried Lucentio, Bianca's husband.

"Content," cried the others.

Then Lucentio sent a message to the fair Bianca bidding her to come to him. And Baptista said he was certain his daughter would come. But the servant coming back, said:

"Sir, my mistress is busy, and she cannot come."

"There's an answer for you," said Petruchio.

"You may think yourself fortunate if your wife does not send you a worse."

"I hope, better," Petruchio answered. Then Hortensio said:

"Go and entreat my wife to come to me at once."

"Oh—if you *entreat* her," said Petruchio.

"I am afraid," answered Hortensio, sharply, "do what you can, yours will not be entreated."

But now the servant came in, and said:

"She says you are playing some jest, she will not come."

"Better and better," cried Petruchio; "now go to your mistress and say I *command* her to come to me."

They all began to laugh, saying they knew what her answer would be, and that she would not come.

Then suddenly Baptista cried:

"Here comes Katharine!" And sure enough—there she was.

"What do you wish, sir?" she asked her husband.

"Where are your sister and Hortensio's wife?"

"Talking by the parlor fire."

"Fetch them here."

When she was gone to fetch them, Lucentio said:

"Here is a wonder!"

"I wonder what it means," said Hortensio.

"It means peace," said Petruchio, "and love, and quiet life."

"Well," said Baptista, "you have won the wager, and I will add another twenty thousand crowns to her dowry—another dowry for another daughter—for she is as changed as if she were some one else."

So Petruchio won his wager, and had in Katharine always a loving wife and a true, and now he had broken her proud and angry spirit he loved her well, and there was nothing ever but love between those two. And so they lived happy ever afterwards.

Hamlet: "Where wilt thou lead me? Speak, I'll go no further"

Hamlet, Prince of Denmark

HAMLET was the only son of the King of Denmark. He loved his father and mother dearly—and was happy in the love of a sweet lady named Ophelia. Her father, Polonius, was the King's Chamberlain.

While Hamlet was away studying at Wittenberg, his father died. Young Hamlet hastened home in great grief to hear that a serpent had stung the King, and that he was dead. The young prince had loved his father tenderly—so you may judge what he felt when he found that the Queen, before yet the King had been laid in the ground a month, had determined to marry again—and to marry the dead King's brother.

Hamlet refused to put off his mourning for the wedding.

"It is not only the black I wear on my body," he said, "that proves my loss. I wear mourning in my heart for my dead father. His son at least remembers him, and grieves still."

Then said Claudius, the King's brother, "This grief is unreasonable. Of course you must sorrow at the loss of your father, but—"

"Ah," said Hamlet, bitterly, "I cannot in one little month forget those I love."

With that the Queen and Claudius left him, to make merry over their wedding, forgetting the poor good King who had been so kind to them both.

And Hamlet, left alone, began to wonder and to question as to what he ought to do. For he could not believe the story about the snake-bite. It seemed to him all too plain that the wicked Claudius had killed the King, so as to get the crown and marry the Queen. Yet he had no proof, and could not accuse Claudius.

And while he was thus thinking came Horatio, a fellow student of his, from Wittenberg.

"What brought you here?" asked Hamlet, when he had greeted his friend kindly.

"I came, my lord, to see your father's funeral."

"I think it was to see my mother's wedding," said Hamlet, bitterly. "My father! We shall not look upon his like again."

"My lord," answered Horatio, "I think I saw him yester-night."

Then, while Hamlet listened in surprise, Horatio told how he, with two gentlemen of the guard, had seen the King's ghost on the battlements. Hamlet went that night, and true enough, at midnight, the ghost of the King, in the armor he had been wont to wear, appeared on the battlements in the chill moonlight. Hamlet was a brave youth. Instead of running away from the ghost he spoke to it—and when it beckoned him he followed it to a quiet place, and there the ghost told him that what he had suspected was true. The wicked Claudius had indeed killed his good brother the King, by dropping poison into his ear as he slept in his orchard in the afternoon.

"And you," said the ghost, "must avenge this cruel murder —on my wicked brother. But do nothing against the Queen, for I have loved her, and she is thy mother. Remember me."

Then seeing the morning approach, the ghost vanished.

"Now," said Hamlet, "there is nothing left but revenge. Remember thee—I will remember nothing else—books, pleasure, youth—let all go—and your commands alone live on my brain."

So when his friends came back he made them swear to keep the secret of the ghost, and then went in from the battlements, now gray with mingled dawn and moonlight, to think how he might best avenge his murdered father.

The shock of seeing and hearing his father's ghost made him feel almost mad, and for fear that his uncle might notice that he was not himself, he determined to hide his mad longing for revenge under a pretended madness in other matters.

And when he met Ophelia, who loved him—and to whom

he had given gifts, and letters, and many loving words—he behaved so wildly to her, that she could not but think him mad. For she loved him so that she could not believe he would be so cruel as this, unless he were quite mad. So she told her father, and showed him a pretty letter from Hamlet. And in the letter was much folly, and this pretty verse:

> *"Doubt that the stars are fire;*
> *Doubt that the sun doth move;*
> *Doubt truth to be a liar;*
> *But never doubt I love."*

And from that time everyone believed that the cause of Hamlet's supposed madness was love.

Poor Hamlet was very unhappy. He longed to obey his father's ghost—and yet he was too gentle and kindly to wish to kill another man, even his father's murderer. And sometimes he wondered whether, after all, the ghost spoke truly.

Just at this time some actors came to the Court, and Hamlet ordered them to perform a certain play before the King and Queen. Now, this play was the story of a man *who had been murdered in his garden by a near relation, who afterwards married the dead man's wife.*

You may imagine the feelings of the wicked King, as he sat on his throne, with the Queen beside him and all his Court around, and saw, acted on the stage, the very wickedness that

he had himself done. And when, in the play, the wicked relation poured poison into the ear of the sleeping man, the
wicked Claudius suddenly rose, and staggered from the room
—the Queen and others following.

Then said Hamlet to his friends, "Now I am sure the ghost
spoke true. For if Claudius had not done this murder, he could
not have been so distressed to see it in a play."

Now the Queen sent for Hamlet, by the King's desire, to
scold him for his conduct during the play, and for other matters; and Claudius wishing to know exactly what happened,
told old Polonius to hide himself behind the hangings in the
Queen's room. And as they talked, the Queen got frightened
at Hamlet's rough, strange words, and cried for help, and
Polonius, behind the curtain, cried out too. Hamlet, thinking
it was the King who was hidden there, thrust with his sword
at the hangings, and killed, not the King, but poor old
Polonius.

So now Hamlet had offended his uncle and his mother,
and by bad hap killed his true love's father.

"Oh, what a rash and bloody deed is this!" cried the Queen.

And Hamlet answered bitterly. "Almost as bad as to kill a
king, and marry his brother." Then Hamlet told the Queen
plainly all his thoughts, and how he knew of the murder, and
begged her, at least, to have no more friendship or kindness

for the base Claudius, who had killed the good King. And as they spoke the King's ghost again appeared before Hamlet, but the Queen could not see it. So when the ghost was gone, they parted.

When the Queen told Claudius what had passed, and how Polonius was dead, he said, "This shows plainly that Hamlet is mad, and since he has killed the chancellor, it is for his own safety that we must carry out our plan, and send him away to England."

So Hamlet was sent, under charge of two courtiers who served the King, and these bore letters to the English Court, requiring that Hamlet should be put to death. But Hamlet had the good sense to get at these letters, and put in others instead, with the names of the two courtiers who were so ready to betray him. Then, as the vessel went to England, Hamlet escaped on board a pirate ship, and the two wicked courtiers left him to his fate, and went on to meet theirs.

Hamlet hurried home, but in the meantime a dreadful thing had happened. Poor pretty Ophelia, having lost her lover and her father, lost her wits too, and went in sad madness about the Court, with straws, and weeds, and flowers in her hair, singing strange scraps of song, and talking poor, foolish, pretty talk with no heart of meaning to it. And one day, coming to a stream where willows grew, she tried to hang a flowery garland on a willow, and fell in the water with all her flowers, and so died.

And Hamlet had loved her, though his plan of seeming madness had made him hide it; and when he came back, he found the King and Queen, and the Court, weeping at the funeral of his dear love and lady.

Ophelia's brother, Laertes, had also just come to Court to ask justice for the death of his father, old Polonius; and now, wild with grief, he leaped into his sister's grave, to clasp her in his arms once more.

"I loved her more than forty thousand brothers," cried Hamlet, and leaped into the grave after him, and they fought till they were parted.

Afterwards Hamlet begged Laertes to forgive him.

"I could not bear," he said, "that any, even a brother, should seem to love her more than I."

But the wicked Claudius would not let them be friends. He told Laertes how Hamlet had killed old Polonius, and between them they made a plot to slay Hamlet by treachery.

Laertes challenged him to a fencing match, and all the Court were present. Hamlet had the blunt foil always used in fencing, but Laertes had prepared for himself a sword, sharp, and tipped with poison. And the wicked King had made ready a bowl of poisoned wine, which he meant to give poor

Hamlet when he should grow warm with the sword play, and should call for drink.

So Laertes and Hamlet fought, and Laertes, after some fencing, gave Hamlet a sharp sword thrust. Hamlet, angry at this treachery—for they had been fencing, not as men fight, but as they play—closed with Laertes in a struggle; both dropped their swords, and when they picked them up again, Hamlet, without noticing it, had exchanged his own blunt sword for Laertes' sharp and poisoned one. And with one thrust of it he pierced Laertes, who fell dead by his own treachery.

At this moment the Queen cried out, "The drink, the drink! Oh, my dear Hamlet! I am poisoned!"

She had drunk of the poisoned bowl the King had prepared for Hamlet, and the King saw the Queen, whom, wicked as he was, he really loved, fall dead by his means.

Then Ophelia being dead, and Polonius, and the Queen, and Laertes, besides the two courtiers who had been sent to England, Hamlet at last got him courage to do the ghost's bidding and avenge his father's murder—which, if he had found the heart to do long before, all these lives had been spared, and none suffered but the wicked King, who well deserved to die.

Hamlet, his heart at last being great enough to do the deed

he ought, turned the poisoned sword on the false King.

"Then—venom—do thy work!" he cried, and the King died.

So Hamlet in the end kept the promise he had made his father. And all being now accomplished, he himself died. And those who stood by saw him die, with prayers and tears for his friends, and his people who loved him with their whole hearts. Thus ends the tragic tale of Hamlet, Prince of Denmark.

Twelfth Night

ORSINO, the Duke of Illyria, was deeply in love with a beautiful Countess, named Olivia. Yet was all his love in vain, for she disdained his suit; and when her brother died, she sent back a messenger from the Duke, bidding him tell his master that for seven years she would not let the very air behold her face, but that, like a nun, she would walk veiled; and all this for the sake of a dead brother's love, which she would keep fresh and lasting in her sad remembrance.

The Duke longed for someone to whom he could tell his sorrow, and repeat over and over again the story of his love. And chance brought him such a companion. For about this time a goodly ship was wrecked on the Illyrian coast, and among those who reached land in safety were the Captain and a fair young maid, named Viola. But she was little grateful for being rescued from the perils of the sea, since she feared that her twin brother was drowned, Sebastian, as dear to her as the heart in her bosom, and so like her that, but for the difference in their manner of dress, one could hardly be told from the other. The Captain, for her comfort, told her that he had seen her brother bind himself to a strong mast that lived upon the sea, and that thus there was hope that he might be saved.

Viola now asked in whose country she was, and learning that the young Duke Orsino ruled there, and was as noble in his nature as in his name, she decided to disguise herself in male attire, and seek for employment with him as a page.

In this she succeeded, and now from day to day she had to listen to the story of Orsino's love. At first she sympathized very truly with him, but soon her sympathy grew to love. At last it occurred to Orsino that his hopeless love-suit might prosper better if he sent this pretty lad to woo Olivia for him. Viola unwillingly went on this errand, but when she came to the house, Malvolio, Olivia's steward, a vain, officious man, sick, as his mistress told him, of self-love, forbade the messenger admittance. Viola, however, (who was now called Cesario) refused to take any denial, and vowed to have speech with the Countess. Olivia, hearing how her instructions were defied and curious to see this daring youth, said, "We'll once more hear Orsino's embassy."

When Viola was admitted to her presence and the servants had been sent away, she listened patiently to the reproaches which this bold messenger from the Duke poured upon her, and listening she fell in love with the supposed Cesario; and when Cesario had gone, Olivia longed to send some love-token after him. So, calling Malvolio, she bade him follow the boy.

"He left this ring behind him," she said, taking one from her finger. "Tell him I will none of it."

Malvolio did as he was bid, and then Viola, who of course knew perfectly well that she had left no ring behind her, saw with a woman's quickness that Olivia loved her. Then she went back to the Duke, very sad at heart for her lover, and for Olivia, and for herself.

It was but cold comfort she could give Orsino, who now sought to ease the pangs of despised love by listening to sweet music, while Cesario stood by his side. "Ah," said the Duke to his page that night, "you too have been in love."

"A little," answered Viola.

"What kind of woman is it?" he asked.

"Of your complexion," she answered.

"What years, i' faith?" was his next question.

To this came the pretty answer, "About your years, my lord."

"Too old, by Heaven!" cried the Duke. "Let still the woman take an elder than herself."

And Viola very meekly said, "I think it well, my lord."

By and by Orsino begged Cesario once more to visit Olivia and to plead his love-suit. But she, thinking to dissuade him, said:

"If some lady loved you as you love Olivia?"

"Ah! that cannot be," said the Duke.

"But I know," Viola went on, "what love woman may have for a man. My father had a daughter loved a man, as it might be," she added blushing, "perhaps, were I a woman, I should love your lordship."

"And what is her history?" he asked.

"A blank, my lord," Viola answered. "She never told her love, but let concealment like a worm in the bud feed on her damask cheek; she pined in thought, and with a green and yellow melancholy she sat, like Patience on a monument, smiling at grief. Was not this love indeed?"

"But died thy sister of her love, my boy?" the Duke asked; and Viola, who had all the time been telling her own love for him in this pretty fashion, said:

"I am all the daughters my father has and all the brothers— Sir, shall I go to the lady?"

"To her in haste," said the Duke, at once forgetting all about the story, "and give her this jewel."

So Viola went, and this time poor Olivia was unable to

hide her love, and openly confessed it with such passionate truth, that Viola left her hastily, saying:

"Nevermore will I deplore my master's tears to you."

But in vowing this, Viola did not know the tender pity she would feel for other's suffering. So when Olivia, in the violence of her love, sent a messenger, praying Cesario to visit her once more, Cesario had no heart to refuse the request.

But the favors which Olivia bestowed upon this mere page aroused the jealousy of Sir Andrew Aguecheek, a foolish, rejected lover of hers, who at that time was staying at her house with her merry old uncle Sir Toby. This same Sir Toby dearly loved a practical joke, and knowing Sir Andrew to be an arrant coward, he thought that if he could bring off a duel between him and Cesario, there would be brave sport indeed. So he induced Sir Andrew to send a challenge, which he himself took to Cesario. The poor page, in great terror, said:

"I will return again to the house, I am no fighter."

"Back you shall not to the house," said Sir Toby, "unless you fight me first."

And as he looked a very fierce old gentleman, Viola thought it best to await Sir Andrew's coming; and when he at last made his appearance, in a great fright, if the truth had been known, she trembling drew her sword, and Sir Andrew in like fear followed her example. Happily for them both, at this moment some officers of the Court came on the scene, and stopped the intended duel. Viola gladly made off with what speed she might, while Sir Toby called after her:

"A very paltry boy, and more a coward than a hare!"

Now, while these things were happening, Sebastian had escaped all the dangers of the deep, and had landed safely in Illyria, where he determined to make his way to the Duke's Court. On his way thither he passed Olivia's house just as Viola had left it in such a hurry, and whom should he meet but Sir Andrew and Sir Toby? Sir Andrew, mistaking Sebastian for the cowardly Cesario, took his courage in both hands, and walking up to him struck him, saying, "There's for you."

"Why, there's for you; and there, and there!" said Sebastian, hitting back a great deal harder, and again and again, till Sir Toby came to the rescue of his friend. Sebastian, however, tore himself free from Sir Toby's clutches, and drawing his sword would have fought them both, but that Olivia herself, having heard of the quarrel, came running in, and with many reproaches sent Sir Toby and his friend away. Then turning to Sebastian, whom she too thought to be Cesario, she besought him with many a pretty speech to come into the house with her.

Sebastian, half dazed and all delighted with her beauty and

grace, readily consented, and that very day, so great was Olivia's haste, they were married before she had discovered that he was not Cesario, or Sebastian was quite certain whether or not he was in a dream.

Meanwhile Orsino, hearing how ill Cesario sped with Olivia, visited her himself, taking Cesario with him. Olivia met them before her door, and seeing, as she thought, her husband there, reproached him for leaving her, while to the Duke she said that his suit was as fat and wholesome to her as howling after music.

"Still so cruel?" said Orsino.

"Still so constant," she answered.

Then Orsino's anger growing to cruelty, he vowed that, to be revenged on her, he would kill Cesario, whom he knew she loved. "Come, boy," he said to the page.

And Viola, following him as he moved away, said, "I, to do you rest, a thousand deaths would die."

A great fear took hold on Olivia, and she cried aloud, "Cesario, husband, stay!"

"Her husband?" asked the Duke angrily.

"No, my lord, not I," said Viola.

"Call forth the holy father," cried Olivia.

And the priest who had married Sebastian and Olivia, coming in, declared Cesario to be the bridegroom.

"O thou dissembling cub!" the Duke exclaimed. "Farewell, and take her, but go where thou and I henceforth may never meet."

At this moment Sir Andrew came up with bleeding crown, complaining that Cesario had broken his head, and Sir Toby's as well.

"I never hurt you," said Viola, very positively; "you drew your sword on me, but I bespoke you fair, and hurt you not."

Yet, for all her protesting, no one there believed her; but all their thoughts were on a sudden changed to wonder, when Sebastian came in.

"I am sorry, madam," he said to his wife, "I have hurt your kinsman. Pardon me, sweet, even for the vows we made each other so late ago."

"One face, one voice, one habit, and two persons!" cried the Duke, looking first at Viola, and then at Sebastian.

"An apple cleft in two," said one who knew Sebastian, "is not more twin than these two creatures. Which is Sebastian?"

"I never had a brother," said Sebastian. "I had a sister, whom the blind waves and surges have devoured. Were you a woman," he said to Viola, "I should let my tears fall upon your cheek, and say, 'Thrice welcome, drowned Viola!'"

Then Viola, rejoicing to see her dear brother alive, confessed that she was indeed his sister, Viola. As she spoke, Orsino felt the pity that is akin to love.

"Boy," he said, "thou hast said to me a thousand times thou never shouldst love woman like to me."

"And all those sayings will I over-swear," Viola replied, "and all those swearings keep true."

"Give me thy hand," Orsino cried in gladness. "Thou shalt be my wife, and my fancy's queen."

Thus was the gentle Viola made happy, while Olivia found in Sebastian a constant lover, and a good husband, and he in her a true and loving wife.

Rosalind. Celia in the Forest of Arden

As You Like It

THERE was once a wicked Duke named Frederick, who took the dukedom that should have belonged to his brother, and kept it for himself, sending his brother into exile. His brother went into the Forest of Arden, where he lived the life of a bold forester, as Robin Hood did in Sherwood Forest in England.

The banished Duke's daughter, Rosalind, remained with Celia, Frederick's daughter, and the two loved each other more than most sisters. One day there was a wrestling match at Court, and Rosalind and Celia went to see it. Charles, a celebrated wrestler, was there, who had killed many men in contests of this kind. The young man he was to wrestle with was so slender and youthful, that Rosalind and Celia thought he would surely be killed, as others had been; so they spoke to him, and asked him not to attempt so dangerous an adventure; but the only effect of their words was to make him wish to come off well in the encounter, so as to win praise from such sweet ladies.

Orlando, like Rosalind's father, was being kept out of his inheritance by his brother, and was so sad at his brother's unkindness that until he saw Rosalind, he did not care much whether he lived or died. But now the sight of the fair Rosalind gave him strength and courage, so that he did marvelously, and at last, threw Charles to such a tune, that the wrestler had to be carried off the ground. Duke Frederick was pleased with his courage, and asked his name.

"My name is Orlando, and I am the youngest son of Sir Rowland de Boys," said the young man.

Now Sir Rowland de Boys, when he was alive, had been a good friend to the banished Duke, so that Frederick heard with regret whose son Orlando was, and would not befriend him, and went away in a very bad temper. But Rosalind was delighted to hear that this handsome young stranger was the son of her father's old friend, and as they were going away, she turned back more than once to say another kind word to the brave young man.

"Gentleman," she said, giving him a chain from her neck, "wear this for me. I could give more, but that my hand lacks means."

Then when she was going, Orlando could not speak, so much was he overcome by the magic of her beauty; but when she was gone, he said, "I wrestled with Charles, and overthrew him, and now I myself am conquered. Oh, heavenly Rosalind!''

Rosalind and Celia, when they were alone, began to talk about the handsome wrestler, and Rosalind confessed that she loved him at first sight.

"Come, come," said Celia, "wrestle with thy affections."

"Oh," answered Rosalind, "they take the part of a better wrestler than myself. Look, here comes the Duke."

"With his eyes full of anger," said Celia.

"You must leave the Court at once," he said to Rosalind.

"Why?" she asked.

"Never mind why," answered the Duke, "you are banished."

"Pronounce that sentence then on me, my lord," said Celia. "I cannot live out of her company."

"You are a foolish girl," answered her father. "You, Rosalind, if within ten days you are found within twenty miles of my Court, you die."

So Rosalind set out to seek her father, the banished Duke, in the Forest of Arden. Celia loved her too much to let her go alone, and as it was rather a dangerous journey, Rosalind, being the taller, dressed up as a young countryman, and her cousin as a country girl, and Rosalind said that she would be called Ganymede, and Celia, Aliena. They were very tired when at last they came to the Forest of Arden, and as they were sitting on the grass, almost dying with fatigue, a country-man passed that way, and Ganymede asked him if he could get them food. He did so, and told them that a shepherd's flocks and house were to be sold. They bought these with the money they had brought with them, and settled down as shepherd and shepherdess in the forest.

In the meantime, Orlando's brother, Oliver, having sought to take his life, Orlando also wandered into the forest, and there met with the rightful Duke, and being kindly received, stayed with him. Now, Orlando could think of nothing but Rosalind, and he went about the forest, carving her name on trees, and writing love sonnets and hanging them on the bushes, and there Rosalind and Celia found them. One day Orlando met them, but he did not know Rosalind in her boy's clothes, though he liked the pretty shepherd youth, because he fancied a likeness in him to her he loved.

"There is a foolish lover," said Rosalind, "who haunts these woods and hangs sonnets on the trees. If I could find him, I would soon cure him of his folly."

Orlando confessed that he was this foolish lover, and Rosalind said, "If you will come and see me every day, I will pretend to be Rosalind, and you shall come and court me, as you would if I were really your lady; and I will take her part, and be wayward and contrary, as is the way of women, till I make you ashamed of your folly in loving her."

And so every day he went to her house, and took a pleasure in saying to her all the pretty things he would have said to Rosalind; and she had the fine and secret joy of knowing that all his love-words came to the right ears. Thus many days passed pleasantly away.

Rosalind met the Duke one day, and the Duke asked her what family "he came from." And Rosalind, forgetting that she was dressed as a peasant boy, answered that she came of as good parentage as the Duke did, which made him smile.

One morning, as Orlando was going to visit Ganymede, he saw a man asleep on the ground, and a large serpent had wound itself round his neck. Orlando came nearer, and the serpent glided away. Then he saw that there was a lioness crouching near, waiting for the man who was asleep, to wake: for they say that lions will not prey on anything that is dead or sleeping. Then Orlando looked at the man, and saw that it was his wicked brother, Oliver, who had tried to take his life. At first he thought to leave him to his fate, but the faith and honor of a gentleman withheld him from this wickedness. He fought with the lioness and killed her, and saved his brother's life.

While Orlando was fighting the lioness, Oliver woke to see his brother, whom he had treated so badly, saving him from a wild beast at the risk of his own life. This made him repent of his wickedness, and he begged Orlando's pardon with many tears, and from thenceforth they were dear brothers. The lioness had wounded Orlando's arm so much, that he could not go on to see the shepherd, so he sent his brother to ask Ganymede ("whom I do call my Rosalind," he added) to come to him.

Oliver went and told the whole story to Ganymede and Aliena, and Aliena was so charmed with his manly way of confessing his faults, that she fell in love with him at once. But when Ganymede heard of the danger Orlando had been in, she fainted; and when she came to herself, said truly enough, "I should have been a woman by right." Oliver went back to his brother and told him all this, saying, "I love Aliena so well, that I will give up my estates to you and marry her, and live here as a shepherd."

"Let your wedding be tomorrow," said Orlando, "and I will ask the Duke and his friends. Go to the shepherdess— she is alone, for here comes her brother."

And sure enough Ganymede was coming through the wood towards them. When Orlando told Ganymede how his brother was to be married on the morrow, he added: "Oh, how bitter a thing it is to look into happiness through another man's eyes."

Then answered Rosalind, still in Ganymede's dress and speaking with his voice, "If you do love Rosalind so near the heart, then when your brother marries Aliena, shall you marry her. I will set her before your eyes, human as she is, and without any danger."

"Do you mean it?" cried Orlando.

"By my life I do," answered Rosalind. "Therefore, put on your best array and bid your friends to come, for if you will be married tomorrow, you shall,—and to Rosalind, if you will."

Now the next day the Duke and his followers, and Orlando, and Oliver, and Aliena, were all gathered together for the wedding.

"Do you believe, Orlando," said the Duke, "that the boy can do all that he has promised?"

"I sometimes do believe and sometimes do not," said Orlando.

Then Ganymede came in and said to the Duke, "If I bring in your daughter Rosalind, will you give her to Orlando?"

"That I would," said the Duke, "if I had all kingdoms to give with her."

"And you say you will have her when I bring her?" she said to Orlando.

"That would I," he answered, "were I king of all kingdoms."

Then Rosalind and Celia went out, and Rosalind put on her pretty woman's clothes again, and after a while came back.

She turned to her father—"I give myself to you, for I am yours."

"If there be truth in sight," he said, "you are my daughter."

Then she said to Orlando, "I give myself to you, for I am yours."

"If there be truth in sight," he said, "you are my Rosalind."

"I will have no father if you be not he," she said to the Duke, and to Orlando, "I will have no husband if you be not he."

So Orlando and Rosalind were married, and Oliver and Celia, and they lived happy ever after, returning with the Duke to the dukedom. For Frederick had been shown by a holy hermit the wickedness of his ways, and so gave back the dukedom of his brother, and himself went into a monastery to pray for forgiveness.

The wedding was a merry one, in the mossy glades of the forest, where the green leaves danced in the sun, and the birds sang their sweetest wedding hymns for the new-married folk. A shepherd and shepherdess who had been friends with Rosalind, when she was herself disguised as a shepherd, were married on the same day, and all with such pretty feastings and merrymakings as could be nowhere within four walls, but only in the beautiful green-wood.

This is one of the songs which Orlando made about his Rosalind:

> *From the east to western Ind,*
> *No jewel is like Rosalind.*
> *Her worth, being mounted on the wind,*
> *Through all the world bears Rosalind.*
> *All the pictures, fairest lin'd*
> *Are but black to Rosalind.*
> *Let no face be kept in mind,*
> *But the fair of Rosalind.*

The grieving Pericles, aboard his barge, approaches Mitylene

Pericles

PERICLES, the Prince of Tyre, was
unfortunate enough to make an enemy of Antiochus, the pow-
erful and wicked King of Antioch; and so great was the danger
in which he stood that, on the advice of his trusty counsellor,
Lord Helicanus, he determined to travel about the world for
a time. He came to this decision despite the fact that, by the
death of his father, he was now King of Tyre. So he set sail
for Tarsus, appointing Helicanus Regent during his absence.
That he did wisely in thus leaving his kingdom was soon made
clear.

Hardly had he sailed on his voyage, when Lord Thaliard
arrived from Antioch with instructions from his royal master
to kill Pericles. The faithful Helicanus soon discovered the
deadly purpose of this wicked lord, and at once sent messengers to Tarsus to warn the king of the danger which threat-
ened him.

The people of Tarsus were in such poverty and distress
that Pericles, feeling that he could find no safe refuge there,

put to sea again. But a dreadful storm overtook the ship in which he was, and the good vessel was wrecked and split to pieces, while of all on board only Pericles was saved, and he in sorry plight indeed. Bruised and wet and faint, he was flung upon the cruel rocks on the coast of Pentapolis, the country of the good King Simonides. Worn out as he was, he looked for nothing but death, and that speedily. But some fishermen, coming down to the beach, found him there, and gave him clothes and bade him be of good cheer.

"Thou shalt come home with me," said one of them, "and we will have flesh for holidays, fish for fasting days, and moreo'er, puddings and flapjacks, and thou shalt be welcome."

Pericles, touched by their kindness, took heart of grace, and the love of life came back to him. They told him that on the morrow many princes and knights were going to the King's Court, there to joust and tourney for the love of his daughter, the beautiful Princess Thaisa.

"Did but my fortunes equal my desires," said Pericles, "I'd wish to make one there."

As he spoke some of the fishermen came by, drawing their net, and it dragged heavily, resisting all their efforts, but at last they hauled it in to find that it contained a suit of rusty armor; and looking at it, he blessed Fortune for her kindness, for he saw that it was his own, which had been given to him by his dead father. He begged the fishermen to let him have it, that he might go to Court and take part in the tournament, promising that if ever his ill fortunes bettered, he would reward them well. The fishermen readily consented, and being thus fully equipped, Pericles set off in his rusty armor to the King's Court. The device on his shield was a withered branch that was only green on the top, and the motto "In hac spe vivo" (In this hope I live).

"A pretty moral," said Simonides to his daughter. "From the dejected state wherein he is, he hopes by you his fortunes yet may flourish."

In the tournament none bore himself so well as Pericles, and he won the wreath of victory, which the fair Princess herself placed on his brows. Then at her father's command she asked him who he was, and whence he came; and he answered that he was a knight of Tyre, by name Pericles, but he did not tell her that he was the King of that country, for he knew that if once his whereabouts became known to Antiochus, his life would not be worth a pin's purchase. Nevertheless Thaisa loved him dearly, and the King was so pleased with his courage and graceful bearing that he gladly permitted his daughter to have her own way, when she told him she would marry the stranger knight or die.

Thus Fortune was kind and gracious to Pericles, and he became the husband of the fair lady for whose sake he had striven with the knights who came in all their bravery to joust and tourney for her love.

Meanwhile the wicked King Antiochus had died, and the people in Tyre, hearing no news of their King, urged Lord Helicanus to ascend the vacant throne. But Helicanus was loyal to his sovereign, and for all their urging they could only get him to promise that he would become their King, if at the end of a year Pericles did not come back. Moreover, he sent forth messengers far and wide in search of the missing Pericles.

Some of these made their way to Pentapolis, and finding their King there, told him how discontented his people were at his long absence, and that, Antiochus being dead, there was nothing now to hinder him from returning to his kingdom. Then Pericles told his wife and father-in-law who he really was, and they and all the subjects of Simonides greatly rejoiced to know that the gallant husband of Thaisa was a King in his own right. So Pericles set sail with his dear wife for his native land.

But once more the sea was cruel to him, for again a dreadful storm broke out, and while it was at its height, a servant came to tell him that a little daughter was born to him. This news would have made his heart glad indeed, but that the servant went on to add that his wife—his dear, dear Thaisa—was dead.

While he was praying the gods to be good to his little baby girl, the sailors came to him, declaring that the dead Queen must be thrown overboard, for they believed that the storm would never cease so long as a dead body remained in the vessel.

Pericles, though he despised their superstitious fears, was obliged to yield to them. So Thaisa was laid in a big chest with spices and jewels, and a scroll on which the sorrowful King wrote these lines:

> " *Here I give to understand,*
> *(If e'er this coffin drive a-land)*
> *I, King Pericles, have lost*
> *This Queen worth all our mundane cost.*
> *Who finds her, give her burying;*
> *She was the daughter of a king;*
> *Besides this treasure for a fee,*
> *The gods requite his charity!*"

Then the chest was cast into the sea, and the waves taking it, by and by washed it ashore at Ephesus, where it was found by the servants of a lord named Cerimon. He at once ordered it to be opened, and when he saw what it held, and how lovely Thaisa looked, he doubted if she were dead, and took im-

mediate steps to restore her. Then a great wonder happened,
for she, who had been thrown into the sea as dead, came back
to life. But feeling sure that she would never see her husband
again, Thaisa retired from the world, and became a priestess
of the goddess Diana.

While these things were happening, Pericles went on to
Tarsus with his little daughter, whom he called Marina, because she had been born at sea. Leaving her in the hands of his
old friend, the Governor of Tarsus, the King sailed for his
own dominions, where his people received him with hearty
welcome.

Now Dionyza, the wife of the Governor of Tarsus, was a
jealous and wicked woman, and finding that the young Princess
grew up a more accomplished and charming girl than her own
daughter, she determined to take Marina's life. So when
Marina was fourteen, Dionyza ordered one of her servants to
take her away and kill her. This villain would have done so,
but that he was interrupted by some pirates who came in and
carried Marina off to sea with them, and took her to Mitylene, where they sold her as a slave. Yet such were her goodness, her grace, and her beauty, that she soon became honored
there, and Lysimachus, the young Governor, fell deep in love
with her, and would have married her, but that he thought

she must be of too humble parentage to become the wife of one in his high position.

The wicked Dionyza believed, from her servant's report, that Marina was really dead, and so she put up a monument to her memory, and showed it to King Pericles, when after long years of absence he came to see his much-loved child. When he heard that she, his only joy in life, was dead, his grief was terrible to see. He set sail once more, and putting on sackcloth, vowed never to wash his face or cut his hair again. There was a pavilion erected on deck and there he lay alone, curtained from the sight of all, and for three months he spoke word to none.

At last it chanced that his ship came into the port of Mitylene, and Lysimachus, the Governor, went on board to inquire whence the vessel came. When he heard the story of Pericles' sorrow and silence, he bethought him of Marina, and, believing that she could rouse the King from his stupor, sent for her and bade her try her utmost to persuade the King to speak, promising whatever reward she would, if she succeeded. Marina gladly obeyed, and sending the rest away, she sat and sang to her poor grief-laden father; yet, sweet as was her voice, he made no sign. So presently she spoke to him, saying that her grief might equal his, if both were justly weighed, and that, though she was a slave, she came from ancestors that stood equivalent with mighty kings.

Something in her voice and story touched the King's heart, and he looked up at her, and as he looked, he saw with wonder how like she was to his lost wife, so with a great hope springing up in his heart, he bade her tell her story.

Then, with many interruptions from the King, she told him who she was and how she had escaped from the cruel Dionyza. So Pericles knew that this was indeed his daughter, and he kissed her again and again, crying that his great seas of joy drowned him with their sweetness. "Give me my robes," he said: "O Heavens, bless my girl!"

Then there came to him, though none else could hear it, the sound of heavenly music, and falling asleep, he beheld the goddess Diana, in a vision.

"Go," she said to him, "to my temple at Ephesus, and when my maiden priests are met together, reveal how thou at sea didst lose thy wife."

Pericles obeyed the goddess and told his tale before her altar. Hardly had he made an end, when the chief priestess, crying out, "You are—you are—O royal Pericles!" fell fainting to the ground, and presently recovering, she spoke again to him, "O my lord, are you not Pericles?"

"The voice of dead Thaisa!" exclaimed the King in wonder.

"That Thaisa am I," she said, and looking at her, he saw that she spoke the very truth, and he called to her:

"O come, be buried a second time in these arms!"

Thus Pericles and Thaisa, after long and bitter suffering, found happiness once more, and in the joy of their meeting they forgot the pain of the past. To Marina great happiness was given, not only in being restored to her dear parents; for she married Lysimachus, and became a princess in the land where she had been sold as a slave.